— Discovering Canada —

Montcalm and Wolfe

Weigl
CALGARY
www.weigl.com

Rebecca Szulhan

Published by Weigl Educational Publishers Limited
6325 10 Street SE
Calgary, Alberta, Canada
T2H 2Z9

Website: www.weigl.com
Copyright ©2009 Weigl Educational Publishers Limited

Library and Archives Canada Cataloguing in Publication data available upon request.
Fax (403) 233-7769 for the attention of the Publishing Records department.

ISBN 978-1-55388-502-3 (hard cover)
ISBN 978-1-55388-503-0 (soft cover)

Printed in the United States of America
1 2 3 4 5 6 7 8 9 0   12 11 10 09 08

We acknowledge the
financial support of the
Government of Canada
through the Book
Publishing Industry
Development Program
(BPIDP) for our
publishing activities.

**PROJECT
COORDINATOR**
Heather C. Hudak

DESIGN
Terry Paulhus

**Photograph credits: Weigl acknowledges Getty Images as the primary image supplier
for this title.**

**Other photograph credits include: Corel Corporation: page 16; Courtesy of New Brunswick
Museum: page 22; Library and Archives of Canada: page 16 (C-1078).**

CONTENTS

Introduction

In the 1700s, both Great Britain and France were involved in the fur trade in what is now Canada. The British established the Hudson's Bay Company, while the French established forts and trading posts along the rivers of **New France**. New France was an important link to trade routes and other resources that were vital to the fur trade. The British started to expand their territory. The inhabitants of New France felt that their land and livelihood were threatened. They thought the British were damaging the fur trade. British and French colonists began fighting.

■ Jacques Cartier was an explorer from France. He claimed the land around the Gulf of St. Lawrence for France.

Explorer Essentials

Europeans began actively exploring North America in the 1400s. At first, they were drawn to the excellent fishing opportunities. People travelled from Europe to North America to fish for cod.

Curiosity about wealth and need for simplified trade routes drove European explorers to sail across the ocean.

1480 Europeans began fishing in North America, including Newfoundland.

1534 Jacques Cartier, the first person to map the Gulf of St. Lawrence, reached present-day Canada.

1605 Samuel de Champlain and Pierre Dugua de Mons founded Port-Royal in present-day Nova Scotia.

Before long, France and Great Britain were also fighting. In 1756, they declared war. A key issue in the Seven Years' War was control over New France. Great Britain was determined to conquer New France and gain control of North America. Each country sent officers to control its troops in New France.

■ During the Seven Years' War, Great Britain, Prussia, and Hanover battled against France, Austria, Sweden, Saxony, Russia, and Spain.

Great Britain sent General James Wolfe to capture New France. France sent General Louis-Joseph Montcalm to resist the British and protect France's interests. Both men were highly regarded officers with distinguished careers. On September 13, 1759, they led their troops into the Battle of the Plains of Abraham. The two nations fought for control of Quebec, a major city in New France.

1608 Samuel de Champlain founded present-day Quebec City.

1670 The land around Hudson Bay and James Bay were claimed for Great Britain by Prince Rupert.

1710 The British captured Port-Royal and Acadia. Port-Royal was renamed Annapolis Royal, and the territory was named Nova Scotia.

1721 Mail service began between two of New France's major settlements, Quebec and Montreal.

1744 The French at Louisbourg attacked the British at Annapolis Royal.

1745 The British military captured Louisbourg.

1748 Louisbourg was returned to the French in a treaty.

1755 The Acadians were expelled from Nova Scotia.

1758 Louisbourg was once again attacked and captured by the British military.

1759 The Battle of the Plains of Abraham was fought. The fate of New France was decided by the outcome of this battle.

Wolfe's Early Years

James Wolfe was born on January 2, 1727, at Westerham, England. Wolfe's mother was Henrietta Thompson. His father was Major-General Edward Wolfe.

As a young boy, Wolfe attended school in Westerham. In 1738, he and his family moved to Greenwich, England, where he continued his studies. Wolfe excelled in mathematics and Latin.

As a child, Wolfe was said to be gentle and sensitive. However, he also was headstrong and determined, with a bit of a temper. He dreamed of joining the military. Wolfe proved himself to be diligent and responsible. He was a natural-born leader who, at 16, confidently assumed positions of command.

■ The Old Royal Naval College is located in Greenwich, England, where Wolfe lived as a child.

In 1740, Wolfe's father, Edward, was a staff officer in the British expedition to Cartagena, Colombia. Wolfe wanted to join his father and planned to volunteer with the expedition. However, he became ill and was unable to go. Throughout his life, Wolfe had to fight against illness. However, he did not let this stop him, and Wolfe went on to lead many successful military campaigns.

Wolfe loved his family. Once he joined the military, he was often away from home. When he was away, he wrote many letters home to his mother and father. He frequently worried about his mother's health, since she often was ill.

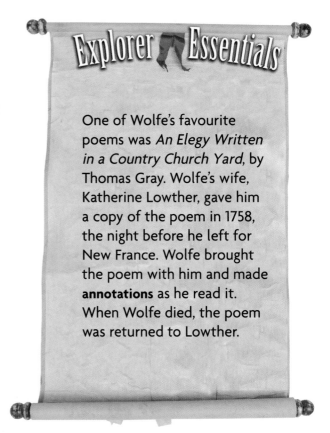

Explorer Essentials

One of Wolfe's favourite poems was *An Elegy Written in a Country Church Yard*, by Thomas Gray. Wolfe's wife, Katherine Lowther, gave him a copy of the poem in 1758, the night before he left for New France. Wolfe brought the poem with him and made **annotations** as he read it. When Wolfe died, the poem was returned to Lowther.

■ Cartagena is located on the northern coast of Colombia. At one time, it was a major trade port. Today, it is a large city seaport.

Montcalm's Early Years

ouis-Joseph de Montcalm-Gozon, Marquis de Saint-Veran was born on February 28, 1712, in the Château of Candiac near Nimes, France. His parents were nobles.

When Montcalm was six years old, he was sent to live with a relative named Dumas. Dumas was a strict man, who made sure that Montcalm studied hard. Montcalm learned Latin, Greek, and history. Sometimes, he was a difficult student who would not listen or take advice. However, Montcalm enjoyed learning, reading, **fencing**, and riding.

By nine years of age, Montcalm had begun his military career. At 12, he became an officer in the French army. Montcalm was a skilled soldier, and he received many promotions and honours. Montcalm's father encouraged his son's blossoming military career. Two years after Montcalm joined the military, his father bought him a promotion to captain.

Montcalm was introduced to Angélique Louise Talon du Boulay by a family friend. Boulay was a wealthy woman with good connections. She and Montcalm were married. They had 10 children, but only six survived.

■ Nimes, where Montcalm was born, is an ancient city that dates back to the Roman Empire.

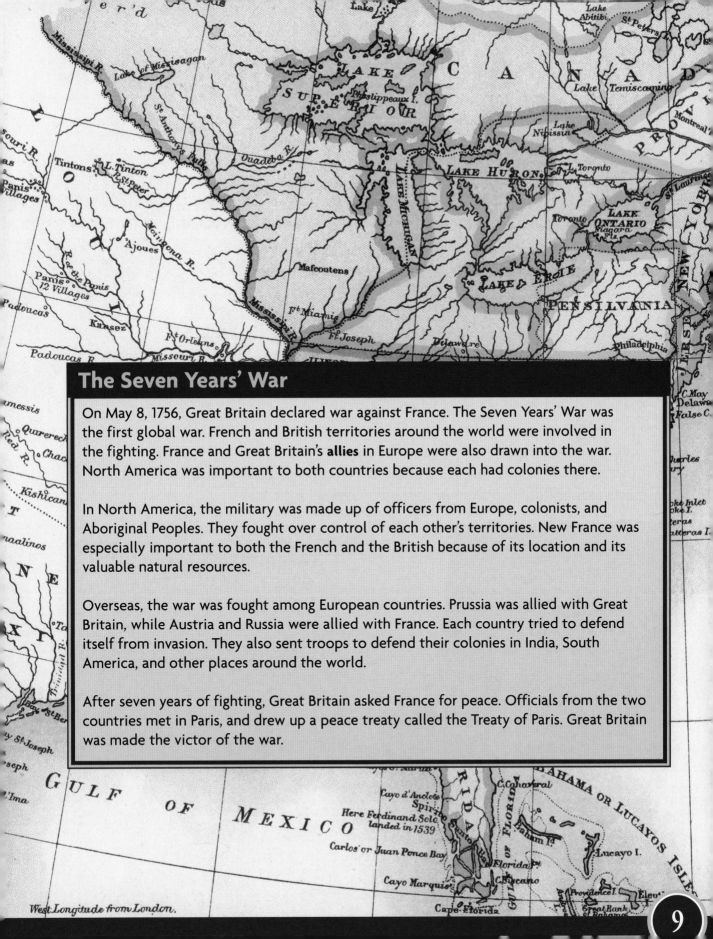

The Seven Years' War

On May 8, 1756, Great Britain declared war against France. The Seven Years' War was the first global war. French and British territories around the world were involved in the fighting. France and Great Britain's **allies** in Europe were also drawn into the war. North America was important to both countries because each had colonies there.

In North America, the military was made up of officers from Europe, colonists, and Aboriginal Peoples. They fought over control of each other's territories. New France was especially important to both the French and the British because of its location and its valuable natural resources.

Overseas, the war was fought among European countries. Prussia was allied with Great Britain, while Austria and Russia were allied with France. Each country tried to defend itself from invasion. They also sent troops to defend their colonies in India, South America, and other places around the world.

After seven years of fighting, Great Britain asked France for peace. Officials from the two countries met in Paris, and drew up a peace treaty called the Treaty of Paris. Great Britain was made the victor of the war.

Early Military Careers

Montcalm became well known as a soldier while fighting in Europe. He took part in the War of Polish Succession and the Austrian War of Succession before he was made a colonel in 1743. Montcalm continued to fight in intense campaigns. While at war in Italy in 1746, Montcalm was cut five times by a sabre, captured, and taken prisoner. When he was released, Montcalm rejoined the military and was promoted to brigadier. Once again, Montcalm was wounded, this time by a musket.

When the war was over, Montcalm was given a **pension** to retire from fighting. He did not fight between 1748 and 1755. Instead, Montcalm spent time with his family and recovering from his ordeals. In 1756, Montcalm was sent to New France to fill in for an officer who had been taken as a prisoner. At first, Montcalm refused the request to go to New France. However, his mother convinced him that it was his duty to go. In 1735, his father died, and Montcalm was left with a large debt. His family's need for money was one of the reasons he agreed to fight in New France.

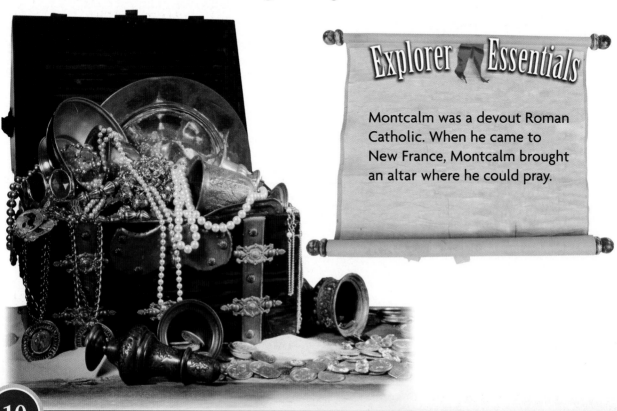

Explorer Essentials

Montcalm was a devout Roman Catholic. When he came to New France, Montcalm brought an altar where he could pray.

Wolfe first joined the military in 1741 as second lieutenant in the 1ˢᵗ Regiment of Marines. His father was the colonel of this regiment. In 1742, Wolfe moved to the 12ᵗʰ Foot, where he was an ensign. The following year, Wolfe fought in the battle of Dettingen in Bavaria. His efforts there earned him a promotion to lieutenant. A year later, Wolfe was made a captain.

After several more battles, Wolfe was made aide-de-camp to Lieutenant-General Henry Hawley in 1746. Wolfe was wounded during the battle of Laffeldt in July of 1747, and took a leave to recover in England. The next year, the Austrian War of Succession ended. Wolfe was appointed major in the 20ᵗʰ Foot and, later, became acting lieutenant-colonel of the regiment.

By 1750, Wolfe was officially made lieutenant-colonel. He entered the Seven Years' War in 1757 as part of the expedition against Rochefort on the French Biscay coast.

■ Although the effort against Rochefort failed, Wolfe was commended for his service. He was promoted to colonel shortly after.

The Bread Protests in New France

The men, women, and children who made New France their home were all affected by the Seven Years' War. One result of the fighting was a food shortage in Quebec. Trying to save money, the governor of New France decided to stop distributing bread. Instead, he wanted people to eat horsemeat and beef, which cost less. People did not like this idea. While the governor was on a trip to Montreal, a group of women went there to protest the bread shortage. The governor threatened to have the women arrested. However, they were not. A few months later, other food supplies in Quebec were running out. The women again held a protest to demand more aid. Ships arrived with much needed supplies. During the winter of 1758 to 1759, wheat supplies had run low, and there was no bread. Four hundred women held a protest. The government sent wheat from Lachine to Quebec and promised to make more bread available in the future.

New France

In 1534, Jacques Cartier sailed across the Atlantic Ocean from France to North America. He landed in present-day Newfoundland and was amazed by the large amounts of cod in the ocean. Cartier knew that fish were an important natural resource and a valuable source of food. That summer, he sailed in the Gulf of St. Lawrence until he reached the Gaspé Peninsula. Cartier knew that the many natural resources of North America would be valuable to France. He claimed the country for France.

In the 1600s, the fur trade became an important industry in North America. The French traded European goods with the Aboriginal Peoples for furs. The furs were then taken back to Europe to make clothing. In 1605, explorer Samuel de Champlain and a group of French fur traders arrived at what is now known as Nova Scotia. They built a settlement at Port-Royal. In 1608, Champlain travelled down the St. Lawrence River and founded a new trading post named Quebec. This marked the beginning of New France. Over the years, missionaries and settlers joined fur traders in this new land. In 1663, New France was declared a royal colony by King Louis XIV. The number of settlers began to increase, as both men and women came to New France.

■ Samuel de Champlain is called the "father of New France" for his part in its settlement.

Wealthy **seigneurs** claimed large areas of land around rivers. **Habitants** farmed land that they rented from seigneurs. Towns began to grow, including Quebec, Montreal, and Trois-Riviéres. The government of New France was located in Quebec. It let the king know the happenings in the royal colony and carried out his orders.

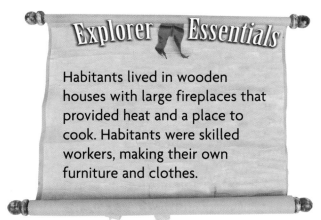

Explorer Essentials

Habitants lived in wooden houses with large fireplaces that provided heat and a place to cook. Habitants were skilled workers, making their own furniture and clothes.

While the French were establishing New France, the British explored other parts of North America. They were also interested in the fur trade, and trading posts were set up at the Hudson Bay and farther west into the Prairies. In the 1700s, Great Britain and France began to fight over control of North America and its resources.

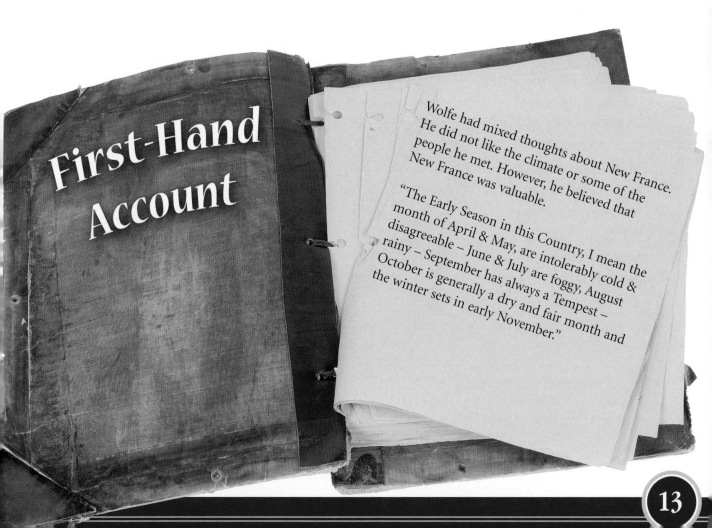

First-Hand Account

Wolfe had mixed thoughts about New France. He did not like the climate or some of the people he met. However, he believed that New France was valuable.

"The Early Season in this Country, I mean the month of April & May, are intolerably cold & disagreeable – June & July are foggy, August rainy – September has always a Tempest – October is generally a dry and fair month and the winter sets in early November."

Tools of the Soldiers

When the British navy sailed from England to New France in 1759, they carried many supplies with them. War materials included 2,000 cannons and 40,000 cannonballs. Surgeons brought medical supplies, and livestock was transported onboard. The 9,000 soldiers and 18,000 sailors were accompanied by their wives and children. Ministers also made the trip to attend to the spiritual needs of the army.

The British light infantry fought mostly in the woods of New France. They needed special clothing. Instead of the hats that other military men wore, they had caps to keep their heads and ears warm. As well, their jackets were shortened so that they could move easier through the forests.

Explorer Essentials

In 1759, soldiers wounded during battle were treated in the same place, whether they were British or French. In fact, deceased French and English soldiers were buried together in the same cemeteries.

■ Since supplies were limited in New France, armies brought many of the goods they needed from Europe.

Officers on both sides of the conflict brought with them items that reminded them of home. Officers carried miniature portraits of important people in their lives. They also brought books or personal items, such as mugs. These things comforted the officers and made their stay in New France more pleasant. Important supplies were ink and **quills**. Soldiers used these tools to write letters home. This was how they communicated with their families and friends in Europe.

Both the British and French troops formed alliances with Aboriginal groups. The Iroquois fought alongside the British. The Algonquin, Huron, and Montagnais Nations allied with the French. The French supplied them with muskets and rifles.

■ The French used cannons to defend New France. Some of their cannons were decorated with engravings. Other weapons used included swords and rifles.

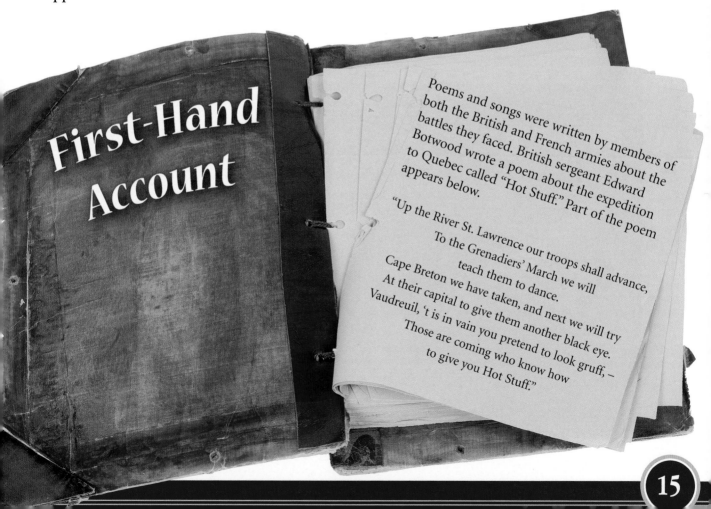

First-Hand Account

Poems and songs were written by members of both the British and French armies about the battles they faced. British sergeant Edward Botwood wrote a poem about the expedition to Quebec called "Hot Stuff." Part of the poem appears below.

"Up the River St. Lawrence our troops shall advance,
To the Grenadiers' March we will
teach them to dance.
Cape Breton we have taken, and next we will try
At their capital to give them another black eye.
Vaudreuil, 't is in vain you pretend to look gruff, –
Those are coming who know how
to give you Hot Stuff."

Wolfe in New France

Wolfe made his first visit to North America in 1758. He, along with Charles Lawrence and Edward Whitmore, were serving as **brigade** commanders under Colonel Jeffrey Amherst on an expedition to capture Louisbourg in present-day Nova Scotia. Wolfe sailed to Halifax on the *Princess Amelia*. He arrived on May 9.

Amherst arrived at Nova Scotia in June. The British ships then sailed to Louisbourg. The weather was very foggy, and the waters were choppy, so they could not get close to the shore. The men had to anchor the ships and wait for five days before they could disembark. Once the weather improved, Amherst led the army to capture Louisbourg.

■ Louisbourg was a strategic fortress built to defend all of the French colonies in New France.

The British military was successful in its attack at Louisbourg. Wolfe and his troops took the fortress. This prevented supplies from reaching the French. Wolfe's role in this expedition became well known and helped build his reputation as an excellent officer. He proved that he had good leadership skills and was reliable. British Prime Minister William Pitt heard of Wolfe's good work. When the time came to attack Quebec, Pitt decided that he wanted Wolfe to command the troops.

Explorer Essentials

Wolfe's death in 1759 inspired several artists. Paintings and drawings of his death drew crowds to galleries. Scenes of his death were even painted on **commemorative** pottery for people's homes.

Wolfe returned to Great Britain after his success at Louisbourg. He needed to recover from injuries he had sustained in the fighting. Wolfe travelled to Bath. There, he met Katherine Lowther, and the pair were soon **betrothed**. Wolfe carried a portrait of Lowther with him until the day he died.

- On 23 January, 1758, William Pitt made Wolfe a brigadier-general and sent him to attack Louisbourg in New France, along with Jeffrey Amherst, a major general.

Montcalm in New France

In New France, Montcalm reported to Governor General Pierre de Rigaud, Sieur de Vaudreuil. Montcalm disliked Vaudreuil. He had little respect for Vaudreuil's abilities, a fact he freely expressed to his superiors. Vaudreuil, in turn, complained about Montcalm's disagreeable and argumentative attitude.

One of Montcalm's first missions was to attack the British Fort Oswego. He reached Oswego on August 10, leading 3,000 men. Four days later, the **garrison** surrendered. Although he was the victor, Montcalm was not pleased with the way that the battle was fought. In New France, **Canadien** militia and Aboriginal Peoples helped French troops stage a series of raids on the British. The goal was to tire out the British and deplete their resources. Montcalm found this way of fighting dishonourable and inefficient. He preferred the European method of two armies fighting large-scale battles in the open.

■ Oswego, a British trading post, was built in 1722. A fort was built at the site five years later.

In 1757, Montcalm thought he deserved a promotion to lieutenant general. Vaudreuil opposed, but the promotion was still granted. Montcalm also asked for a raise in his salary, saying that he was in debt because of his efforts on behalf of the colony. His request was granted.

Montcalm continued to fight in New France. However, he still did not get along with his superior officers. Vaudreuil requested to have Montcalm sent back to France. His said that Aboriginal Peoples and the Canadien militia no longer wanted to take orders from Montcalm because he looked down on them. Vaudreuil's request was denied. Instead, Montcalm was given control over the entire French army in New France. He led the army on campaigns until the summer of 1759, when the British arrived at the Plains of Abraham. Montcalm quickly amassed his troops and led them to battle. It was a hasty decision that proved fatal.

■ When Montcalm was not fighting, he enjoyed spending time at home with his mother, wife, and children.

The Battle of the Plains of Abraham

Wolfe first attacked Quebec in the early summer of 1759. At that time, his army was forced to retreat by the stronger French army. On September 13, 1759, he made a second attack at what is now known as Wolfe's Cove. The British climbed over cliffs to reach Quebec and lined up on the Plains of Abraham to wait for the French to awake. Montcalm saw the British soldiers waiting and was shocked and angry to see them so close to Quebec. He took it as an insult and wanted revenge. Montcalm reacted immediately by ordering his troops to attack. The Battle of the Plains of Abraham had begun.

At first, it seemed as though the French troops had a better chance of winning a battle at Quebec than the British. Quebec was surrounded by rivers and cliffs. This made it difficult for attacking troops to reach the city.

■ *A View of the Taking of Québec* is an artist's rendering of the events leading up to and including the Battle of the Plains of Abraham. These events took place over many hours, but the artist has shown them all happening at once.

Montcalm led an army of 16,000 men. Wolfe only had 9,000 men. However, Montcalm decided to engage the British troops impulsively, without proper preparation. Many people believe this decision led to the French army's defeat.

Montcalm gave the order for his army to advance on the British army at 10 a.m. When they were 120 metres from the British troops, the French soldiers opened fire. They were too far away from the British army for their bullets to have any effect. Wolfe told his troops to withhold their fire until the French soldiers were closer. They waited until the French were 12 metres away before opening fire. The French troops were forced to retreat against this assault. The British soldiers pursued, following the French into the brush. There, they met the Canadiens, who ambushed the British soldiers. When the battle was over, less than 30 minutes later, each side had suffered about the same number of **casualties**.

■ Robert Rogers was an American soldier who helped the British during the Seven Years' War.

Victory for the British Military

During the Battle of the Plains of Abraham, both Wolfe and Montcalm were fatally wounded. Wolfe was shot twice. The first time, he was shot in the wrist. He ignored this injury and continued fighting. Shortly after receiving the first wound, he was shot in the chest. Two of Wolfe's loyal soldiers were with him when he was shot. They lowered Wolfe to the ground and stayed with him so he would not be alone. They told Wolfe that the British army was winning the battle. All around them, French soldiers were retreating. Wolfe gave his final order, telling his men to pursue the retreating French soldiers.

Montcalm was wounded at the same time as Wolfe. He was shot in the stomach by a cannonball and was unable to continue fighting. Montcalm's men took him to shelter at Quebec's Upper Town. There, the full extent of his injury was revealed, and the men told Montcalm that he would die from his injury. Montcalm replied, "I am happy I shall not live to see the surrender of Quebec." Vaudreuil wanted to launch an immediate counterattack against the British troops. Montcalm disagreed with this strategy.

- After giving his final order, Wolfe rolled onto his side and spoke his last words, "Now, God be praised, I will die in peace."

He did not think the French were powerful enough to risk another battle. He knew that they could not defeat the British army. From his deathbed, Montcalm wrote to Vaudreuil and declared that the French army should surrender. Vaudreuil complied with Montcalm's request. During the night, the French army retreated. At dawn, September 14, Montcalm died.

Quebec formally surrendered on September 17. After the battle was over, Vaudreuil was blamed for the defeat, since he had officially ordered the surrender. Montcalm was declared a hero for his sacrifice.

Explorer Essentials

At the Battle of the Plains of Abraham, Wolfe led the Louisbourg Grenadiers into battle. This unit was put together especially for fighting at Quebec. The troops came from three British regiments that had fought at Louisbourg, like Wolfe.

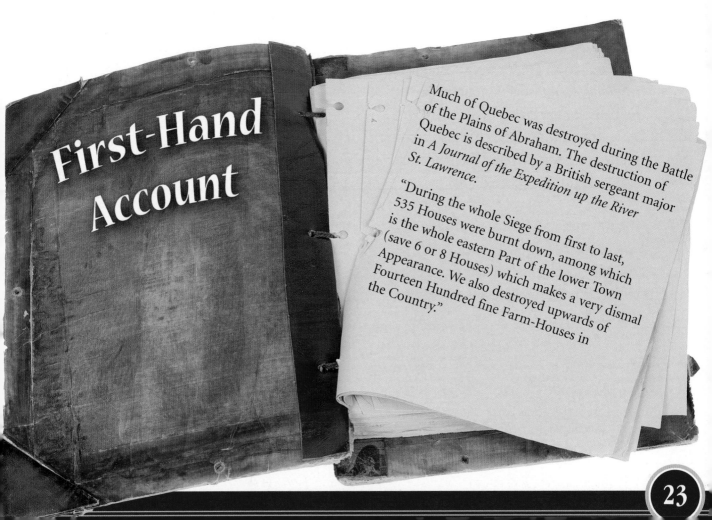

First-Hand Account

Much of Quebec was destroyed during the Battle of the Plains of Abraham. The destruction of Quebec is described by a British sergeant major in *A Journal of the Expedition up the River St. Lawrence.*

"During the whole Siege from first to last, 535 Houses were burnt down, among which is the whole eastern Part of the lower Town (save 6 or 8 Houses) which makes a very dismal Appearance. We also destroyed upwards of Fourteen Hundred fine Farm-Houses in the Country."

Great Britain Claims New France

After the fall of Quebec, it took only a short time for the British army to claim the rest of New France. Great Britain now controlled Quebec and had the more powerful military force. There was still one more battle to be fought, however.

The winter of 1759 to 1760 was cold and harsh. Many French and British soldiers became sick with **dysentery** or **scurvy**. New leaders had taken command of the troops since the death of Wolfe and Montcalm. The French were led by Brigadier-General François-Gaston, Duc de Lévis. Brigadier-General James Murray led the British.

Lévis wanted to retake Quebec. The French attacked, and the British troops defended. Both armies were weakened by the losses they had sustained during the Battle of the Plains of Abraham and by the tough winter they had endured. Neither side was winning the battle and needed reinforcements.

Great Britain and France both sent more soldiers to New France, racing to arrive at Quebec first. Whoever received reinforcements the quickest would win the battle.

■ James Murray was the first British governor of Quebec. He was often caught between those who wanted to assimilate the French Canadians and those who did not.

The first British ship appeared on May 8. The French retreated on May 16, 1670, but were pursued by the British. By early September, Lévis was forced to admit defeat.

When the Treaty of Paris was signed in 1763, France's surrender was official. During the negotiations for the Treaty of Paris, France ceded its claim to New France. It decided instead to keep other territory that it had captured from the British. This was the beginning of British North America.

The British government allowed French Canadians to remain in the province of Quebec. The culture, language, and religion of the French Canadians were protected. The British government wanted to ensure that the French and British inhabitants of Quebec lived together peacefully. They knew that cooperation was important to the settlers' success.

■ Today, Quebec City is the capital of the province of Quebec.

Soldier Expeditions

Many soldiers came to New France to fight for their country's strongholds during the Seven Years' War. Montcalm and Wolfe played key roles in this war.

CANADA

Lake Superior

Lake Huron

Lake Ontario

Oswego

Lake Erie

General Louis-Joseph Montcalm

Montcalm commanded the French army during the Battle of the Plains of Abraham. He died during the fight, and the French eventually lost the battle.

- ☐ Montcalm's First Attack
- ☆ Montcalm Dies

Louisbourg

QUEBEC

Trois-Riviéres

Montreal

General James Wolfe

Wolfe commanded the British army, leading it to victory at the Battle of the Plains of Abraham. Though he died during the fight, the British eventually went on to win the battle.

 Wolfe's First Attack

⭐ Wolfe Dies

Timeline

1712 Louis-Joseph de Montcalm-Gozon, Marquis de Saint-Veran is born in France.

1718 Montcalm is sent to live with Dumas, who becomes his tutor.

1727 James Wolfe is born in Great Britain.

1738 Wolfe moves with his family to Greenwich, England, where he continues his education.

1741 Wolfe joins the military under the leadership of his father.

1746 While fighting in the Austrian War of Succession, Montcalm is injured and taken prisoner.

1747 Wolfe is injured in battle and must take time off from fighting to recover.

1748 After the Austrian War of Succession ends, Montcalm takes a break from the military to recover from his ordeals. He enjoys relaxing with his family.

1756 Montcalm reluctantly returns to battle. He no longer wishes to fight, but his family needs the money.

1758 Wolfe sails to New France for the first time. He takes part in the capture of Louisbourg. Afterward, he returns to Great Britain.

1759 Wolfe is sent to attack Quebec. At dawn on September 13, the Battle of the Plains of Abraham is fought. Both Wolfe and Montcalm are killed. The French are forced to retreat, and the British claim victory.

1760 The French military in New France is commanded by Brigadier-General François-Gaston, Duc de Lévis. The British military in New France is commanded by Brigadier-General James Murray. The French make a last stand at Quebec but admit defeat.

1763 The Treaty of Paris is signed between France and Great Britain. France surrenders New France to Great Britain. Although the French colonists are now ruled by the British government, they keep their language, culture, and religion alive.

- Montcalm died before the French surrendered to Great Britian.

Make Your Own Standard

A standard is a flag with a distinctive picture. Standards are often carried into battle. The pictures and colours on the flags represent the people who made it. You can make your own standard to show what is important to you. You can hang it on your wall as a decoration.

Materials

pre-stretched, pre-primed canvas
oil or acrylic paints
acrylic sealer
an egg carton to mix the paint
a bowl for water

paintbrushes
pencil
ruler
scrap paper

Instructions

1. Decide what you want to put on your standard. Think about what is important to you. What do you want people to know about you? How can you symbolize those things? For example, if you love to read, you might want to put a picture of a book on your standard.
2. Once you have decided what you want to include, you will need to create a design. What is the nicest way to arrange all of the images? Draw some practice pictures on scrap paper.
3. Once you have decided on a design, draw it in pencil on your canvas.
4. Paint the background your favourite colour.
5. Then, paint the images in your design. Use a big brush for wide areas and a small brush for detail.
6. When your painting is dry, spray it with sealer to protect it. Once the sealer is dry, your standard is finished and ready to hang.

Quiz

1. What war was declared in 1756 between France and Great Britain?

2. Why did Montcalm decide to fight in New France in 1756?

3. When did Wolfe first come to New France?

4. Where was the government of New France located?

5. How long did the Battle of the Plains of Abraham last?

6. When did Wolfe and Montcalm die?

7. Who took command of British troops after Wolfe's death?

8. Who led the French after Montcalm died?

9. When did France officially surrender New France to Great Britain?

10. Where was one of Montcalm's first battles in New France?

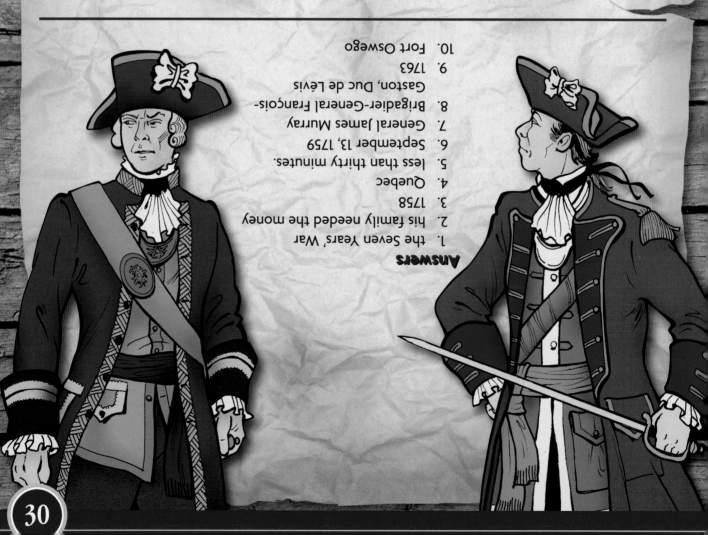

Answers

1. the Seven Years' War
2. his family needed the money
3. 1758
4. Quebec
5. less than thirty minutes.
6. September 13, 1759
7. General James Murray
8. Brigadier-General François-Gaston, Duc de Lévis
9. 1763
10. Fort Oswego

Websites

To learn more about Montcalm, Wolfe, and the Battle of the Plains of Abraham, visit the Virtual Museum at http://1759.ccbn-nbc.gc.ca/index.html

To learn more about Canadian history, including the lives of Wolfe and Montcalm, visit the CBC website at http://history.cbc.ca

Books

Hacker, Carlotta. *The Kids Book of Canadien History*. Toronto: Kids Can Press, 2002.

Livesey, Robert, and A.G. Smith. *New France*. Toronto: Stoddart, 1990.

Glossary

allies: partners, people, or groups who have agreed to work together

annotations: notes

betrothed: to be engaged to be married; the person to whom one is engaged

brigade: a unit in the army that is part of a larger division

Canadien: French colonists who joined the French army

casualties: people who are killed or injured

commemorative: something that celebrates the memory of a person, place, or event

deported: forced to leave

dysentery: an often-fatal disease that upsets the stomach

fencing: sword fighting using special lightweight swords called foils

garrison: the building that troops stay in when they are stationed somewhere; a group of soldiers who are stationed somewhere

habitants: French farmers in New France

New France: the name for the French territories in North America until 1763

pension: an income that someone receives after they retire

quills: feather pens

scurvy: a disease caused by not getting enough vitamin C

seigneurs: wealthy French landowners in New France

Index